Time is Standing Still at a Furious Pace

Aphorisms, Adages, Maxims, Proverbs, Epigrams, Litotes, and Sheer Nonsense

G.J. Violet

Copyright @2022 by G.J. Violet

All rights reserved. No part of this book may be reproduced in any form or by any electronic or mechanical means, including information storage and retrieval systems, without permission in writing from the publisher, except by reviewers, who may quote brief passages in a review.

This publication contains the opinions and ideas of its author. It is intended to provide helpful and informative material on the subjects addressed in the publication. The author and publisher specifically disclaim all responsibility for any liability, loss or risk, personal or otherwise, which is incurred as a consequence, directly or indirectly, of the use and application of any of the contents of this book.

WORKBOOK PRESS LLC
187 E Warm Springs Rd,
Suite B285, Las Vegas, NV 89119, USA

Website: https://workbookpress.com/
Hotline: 1-888-818-4856
Email: admin@workbookpress.com

Ordering Information:
Quantity sales. Special discounts are available on quantity purchases by corporations, associations, and others.
For details, contact the publisher at the address above.

Library of Congress Control Number:
ISBN-13:   978-1-952754-88-3 (Paperback Version)
            978-1-952754-89-0 (Digital Version)

REV. DATE: 10/13/2022

TIME IS STANDING STILL AT A FURIOUS PACE

APHORISMS, ADAGES, MAXIMS, PROVERBS,
EPIGRAMS, LITOTES AND SHEER NONSENSE

by

G.J. Violet

Emotions Transmit Consciousness.

It is amazing how much people will do for people they don't like and how little for people they like so very much.

There is more in nothing than can be found in everything.

The tail of the hummingbird and the tail of the albatross serve the same end.

Only one time therefore only one history.

Reality does not work.

Truth is discernible as it has an effect on the emotions.

Defeat mystery and become great.

Why run before the gun sounds.

or fight before the bell rings.

or sing before the curtain opens.

The great sarcophagus of Ego: The Earth.

Flamingos tall stand flamingo-like in the flaming sun.

A drop of dew is a loaded die.

Love is not a garden that can be tended by a single gardener.

Things break just before you can get to them.

He glowed in the basking of sunlight.

You have to get up bright and stupid in the morning to know the difference between genius and idiocy.

Is Creation a Nightmare that began at the Big Bang?

From pacifiers to placebos to déjà-vu to archetypes ideas follow like clouds in a raging sky.

Whale tears: tears of knowing regret.

The only dream that is not a dream is the dream we are living.

A word is worth a thousand pictures.

Melodic existentialism.

When you validate people, individuals, minorities, you increase the wealth of the state.

Many knock on heaven's door with their favorite religion.

Daffodils, dahlias, gladiolas, hyacinths, narcissuses tulips exhale from the fields of the earth what a mass of detail in life's daily computerization.

Poor people get it in the end right from the very beginning.

The parrot in its cage can only bicker.

Without time no percept.

We perceive in the chemistry of music the physics of paradise.

At the symphony the pregnant silence gave birth to a sextet hat an orgy of sense poetry can hide.

Star Suckers Unite.

They think they are in heaven but all about them hell has broken loose.

Sex Luther is Super Bang's foe.

His permit was suspended for driving one-eyed in a Lada.

In the House of Come-Ons all rose for the National Tantrum.

The cross lies shattered in pieces from one end of history to the other.

When my turn came there was not a ring left on the may pole.

The cock has crowed twice O Man: once at Hiroshima and again at Nagasaki.

The thoughts of others: pebbles at the bottom of the pool.

An orchestra of whales.

A ward for all reasons.

The absurd evidences reality.

It was either a skeletal reversal or a spinal column inversion or a rectal absorption of the skeletal frame.

Polyps in limestone cases.

Let their épaulettes reveal their stars.

When the artist is king the world will be in its glory.

In a battle everyone loses whether they fight or not.

A peacock does not fluff the feathers of another.

Biodegradable relationships.

One put grief and laughter in my bones.

At last, he drank his shadow's flask.

The plight of one is a prophecy to many.

A necklace of pearls and sweet grass.

Does heaven look like hell from outside?

Is the universe playing baseball?

The nightmare wheel continues its dark circle.

We have risen from the grasses only to perish in the grasses.

Humankind is the universe's precipitation.

The datum has been lost in the data.

Time is wisdom aging.

Cheap crooks in the guise of politicians are bagging the continent.

Is that a breeze or an ibis coming down from heaven?

Galactic ships of joy or intelligent sentience burning forever.

What is love unspoken.

Tool less in inutility.

I saw the earth with the eyes of an ape and knew that man came from himself.

Too late I forgot too long I remembered.

Through intellectual consciousness radiate the awareness of the great human mental plane.

To sit saying nothing and manifest the immanifest like a pebble on a rock.

World what time what space what thoughts. Will those who sleep wake up the watchman?

Is rust the entropy of magnetism?

I was delighting in my mentation when there rushed through me a sensation of consciousness enjoying.

This is no place for a shamed man here the tears of the proud fall from heaven like pearls.

Questions crash in upon me like the stars of a million galaxies.

You can't stand on a flower and admire a garden.

Since the state has separated itself from the churches, how can it legislate moral law?

Can the earth generate human life throughout eternity?

Humankind is at war with heaven.

Here is another madman who believes that the rest of the world is crazy.

The conundrum is utterly problematical.

With our puny organs, we can see light years away.

Stars like jellyfish resorb in the galaxy.

You could put it mildly but it would still hurt if you have never done it before.

Though sound is the original of speech silence is the original of sound.

And the universe said: "I made a man who laughs like the devil".

So, what if we destroy life on earth. This solar heaven will regenerate and in hundreds of millions of years our shameful fossils will be unearthed and our civilizations excoriated.

The repression of love leads to war it is a kind of para-philia.

Burp said the bore to the vapor.

Non-compulsive schismaticalness.

Enphlegmed psyches.

Wealthy pseudo-humanists.

A book of chides for April first.

In this so called age of freedom all the aphrodisiacs which were legal in the past thousands of years are now illegal.

People jump from parachute to parachute so often they never reach the ground.

None of us knows what is really going on we all just pretend so as not to look silly.

Inorganophile: one who lusts for materiality.

The character of oneself remains to be seen.

You find us thus O great one, in this Western Armageddon, before the burden you have promised us.

The Universe is an initial motion machine.

You are lucky to be born and you are lucky to die.

We are all part of an invisible movement.

Mathematically we are ghosts.

Terrorized by economic woes many live in a state.

It's of personal emergency equivalent to war not how good you are but how bad you look that matters.

Yuppies: high riders of the worsted plains.

The media have become the Emperors couturiers.

Haley's Comet has drawn all the media hounds in its tail.

We are atoms within atoms within atoms.

Time is so short that you have to travel at the speed of light to catch up to it.

He became an illustrator of conundrums.

Behold the Jujube Witnesses.

What can a nickel get you?

To escape political delusion it is necessary sometimes to become mad.

He has many mansions but can't remember their addresses.

He felt like a mint after a friend told him that he had a knack for coining phrases.

Things thought up are a work of art.

You can't swim in the air nor fly on the sea but what is even more amazing is that you can walk on Earth.

The anthroposophy of knowledge stems from the inner kingdom where the metaphysical experience is divined.

I know now at last that we want to be gods.

For many, capitalism is a horrible personnel experience.

Communication causes emotion.

In rhythm with The Great Day was humankind born.

Billions of birds on the shores of the glacial seas sunbathe.

Politics is an anthill of egos.

You make a Sunday out of every day.

Dam the arrogance of it all.

Consciousness is like a stone which skips upon time's ocean and ripples into infinite space.

The wise like hummingbirds drink-in the succulence of nation.

The human face is an organ of consciousness.

Krishna is an aboriginal deity.

The lucency of these eyes carries into what is around them.

Priests obfuscate the social predilection.

When the prism of the imagination is opened the miraculous will become common.

Oh, to fall in love and to enjoy concupiscence.

An expanded consciousness caused their personality to exude.

In reality ideas have more substance than matter.

The planet Earth is sexuated.

The winds of time carry us once and forever.

She swooned away and quaffed a dram of sleep.

What a ragout of stars!.

A biology of love hidden in the brain.

No king or priest or government can hide from us our ultimate design forever to rid history of its incipient evil and cast out the ancient usurper.

Truth rings loud and clear especially in silence. Can imperfection succeed where perfection failed?

The rich man will take a dollar, the priest a dime, and the pauper a penny.

There are uncanny gaps between the ages.

What was primeval and then medieval has become all evil.

The cataclysm occurred in the chasm.

Time is a drug of infinite sensation.

Every word spoken, every phrase and sentenceuttered is the speech of dreamers dreaming.

They believe that history sleeps and that the awakened nations are evil but the hour of these lands also will come for time will no longer stand still.

Every achievement is a failure and every great achievement is a great failure.

There is a silver lining about the cloud of time.

From the abacus to computers from sparks to shuttles from accidents to madness.

Left alone to my own devices I pursued heaven's interest and found the root.

of the legendary tree upon the shore of time's rocky waters.

No amount of happiness can buy money.

Inexplicably I am not what I am.

Fear not, between coming and becoming there is only a shadow.

A hero is born not of harrowing experiences but of predestined labor.

Why should the price of goods not be based on tradition as is the price of curd in Samarqand.

Is oblivion still a gateway to happiness?

Respect for what is good is great but respect for what is bad is evil.

That king slings curses like a man flings blessings.

Zod's well that zen's well.

Quarantine all nuclear devices.

The subjugation of all private interests to the international good.

The integration of a universal and equitable economy.

Whoever wanted a heaven got a heaven and whoever wanted a hell got a hell.

There is all to physics that meets the eye.

A successful mash of mystical bubblies.

There is no Maharaja, there is no Hinayana, there is only Magnana.

Between drama and trauma there is a curtain.

A cantankerous taciturn.

On the Earth's tombstone stamp: $E = MC2$.

Now there are many mad men who believe that the world has gone crazy.

In 1986 American workers passed water on the Statue of Liberty.

He waits for his day like a boxer for a fight he has yet to be invited to.

May your fate trail in the dragon's dust.

Time's press makes a bitter wine.

Plants are the best furniture.

When outside is inside since inside is outside inside is inside no longer and outside no longer outside.

The most dangerous drugs are the legal ones.

May truth pearl upon your lips.

A world reasonable for love and a love reasonable for the world.

Relations with other people are difficult, one must live them through as best one can.

It took trillions of years to make but it only takes one second to behold it.

Heaven's natural aria can be heard day and night.

The judicial excision of a pretense.

The flower generation was vilified because it represented a New Earth.

Born; I went to heaven.

The existence of humankind is simply the materialization of consciousness according to conditions which it has generated for itself.

All things since time immemorial are stored away in human consciousness.

Everyday billions of dreamers hit the streets of the world.

He purses his brow and the words in his mind spit out like coins at a stockbrokers lunch.

Democracy means that the media can make people elect the devil by calling him god.

From tent to tent love generated family after family time after time until reality became eternal.

Hashishins, Marmaluks and Hijras dwell among us along with myriad others.

I asked and the great one gave in bewildering measure but of that which I perceived none would believe.

Fight the controllers that the politicians have put over us.

Human biology is threefold; mechanical, electrical and metaphysical.

To avoid merit the Buddha did not act having no desire he practiced nothing yet when the stars shone his deed was done.

Pangaea... Eden... Paradise... Earth...

The ego is the perpetrator of karmic deeds and the sole subject of its enlightenment.

Heaven's coin is cheapened by matter.

Roams Chlamydia in herpes land O gonorrhea born?

Deprived of mood we cannot even despair.

Epigrams synalepha synecdoche the secrets of language are a blessing to the cursed.

Para-diabolically the great dragon makes his home in Disneyland.

Thoughts lurk behind the curtain of memory.

The media is an institutionalized deception.

Monoclonal Diaspora.

You have therefore you are you have not therefore you are not.

Governments with pomp and circumstance destroy their peoples only to fatten the accounts of usurers.

Asphyxiate chortle and die.

They gargle with the devil's urine those preachers who have made the bomb their savior and they char the feet of their unholy ghost.

Go ride a satyr.

Bimbopaths.

By the time I remembered I had to forget it.

What is the Earth doing up here anyway?

Nymphomites: Something small.

Your heart, brain and lungs expand and contract your ego.

For a child this is heaven for an adult this hides hell.

Art is the rose which rises out of the political manure of history.

Children live in the mystery of the Earth's silent joy.

The lives of the children of the Earth are in the hands of politicians.

Bums are the dromedaries of the American economic desert.

In a way politics is the end of the world.

Tied to the tide of American Economic Messianism the world sinks deeper and deeper into Hell's cauldron.

Capitalism the poisoned cornucopia.

Christianity today: theocratic capitalism.

When even those who try the most fail no one can raise his or her head.

Liberty is a polemical straight jacket.

The style is an effect of the message.

Einstein: E = MC2 = Bang.

Reality has its own grammar.

There is a place in the mind which is the twin of that place wherein eternity finds its reflection.

Truth in its most simple form is grandiloquent and hard to swallow.

Consciousness is genetically orchestrated.

Love is a theft agreed upon by both parties.

Only Orpheus" armpits can coax Eurydice out of her lunar period.

That's what it's all about and there is nothing else about it at all.

Equal equals equal.

Gold is a pale imitation of love.

From Amadeus to Adolph ...?

In the End everybody will be 66% smaller.

Poetry is a trick for many johns.

RR. = rebel and revolt.

The Earth is peopled with Heaven's people.

Politics is an epoxy of problems stuck together.

The esoteric universe of the mystic land!

Between the problem and its attendant conundrum there is a shadow.

If your face falls your head must follow

There are two currencies in the world: Love and Money.

He walked on a gangplank of gags.

Some fish where most men swim.

Ecology or Ideology.

He fidgets with a rigid digit.

Human consciousness is an outer space experience.

The absurd is the last possible reality.

He who burns lives in the flame of his fire.

Those who live in fear live in their own shadow.

We often are to each other's mind as an absent presence.

When the bow breaks the cradle will fall and down will come baby, politics and all.

It does not look like a Messiah will come and change the irony of fate into a blessing.

I heard from heaven today that all hell is breaking loose.

The main expression of power is arbitrariness.

The best artists are thieves.

The world will stand on its ear.

So what if we totally destroy life on Earth? The solar heaven is eternal. In 500,000 years new life would emerge and the memory of this Earth would be encoded in its genus and species.

There once were noble people on the economic frontier now they are all cruel.

Don't hide feedback.

To loose myself I need no help, to find myself no one can help, I am lost when I am found and found only when I am lost!

You can't stand still and dance at the same time.

Jade green polyps on a bright red stem a new flower blooms in future times.

Our trust in the great One is perfunctory since we let the devil take care of everything.

The imagination of time is stretched beyond limits.

Star filled jellyfish pulse in the galaxy.

Capitalist democracies are fascistic.

I scoff at lovers who impose conditions establish rules and dominate that beast whose burden is love. And I admire those who request conditions, negotiate rules and ride that beast whose passenger is love.

In a land where the law can break the law even the just are guilty.

You can't put a price on great treasures yet the priceless goes begging all the time.

The womb of the beggar women holds heaven's embryo.

While the political shepherds are selling the flock to the butcher, the wolves are eating us one by one.

Like swine they eat the corn of human enslavement.

Fate less and without destiny one is not bound to the inescapable?

I was peering into the everlasting when reality crashed in upon me like a thunderbolt.

When we prevaricate about evil we obviate all that is good.

Their wealth will jell about their knees like a radioactive skirt.

The ill advised rule obstinately.

A crass and ignominious bourgeois pseudo aristocracy.

Reality is an anthropological nightmare.

We voted they won.

But for those aggressive hyperactive boys the meek would rule and do so wisely.

Art is an artphrodisiac.

The day gives back what the night takes away.

Human history appears to be a reprieve from good.

The muscle less bound airhead could barely wreathe or writhe but we voted for him anyway.

Who can forget the sight of a red-breasted cock robin in a crowd of black coated tits.

Extremism in the defense of liberty is no panacea but that is how liberty was obtained to begin with.

Since hell has already frozen over.

It appeared to nature that it was co-evil with eternity, so it secreted causation and time began its contest with eternity.

It's a wicker Emporium and it is rattan to the core.

If it fits use it.

An economist is supposed to be an engineer who builds bridges to prosperity.

A lexical engineer: a poet.

Justice is the law's garter belt.

This is a beautiful place when it spreads its cheeks in sunlight.

In the library men come and go talking of Isaac Asimov.

The only people who do not succumb to flattery are those who are never flattered.

When in doubt put it in the microwave.

Their guns at their temple they looked tragic like Greek gods.

A watt of joy.

Reality is taboo in eternity.

Non-expleted deletives.

Send the progenitor of fishes to another planet.

A supine salmon its belly buried in the pebbles spawns eggs for white people while the nations the Universe first placed here stare from the shore beside their empty canoes.

There are internal organs, external organs and eternal organs.

Good men have the lachrymal glands of women.

With the poor justice easily works its way down but with the rich justice has to work its way up.

The currency of life is love.

Long live the Haida.

The baby-boomers rejected morbid sexual boundaries but it was the pill that loosened them beyond the edge.

Let's raise a stink about pollution.

Like turtles we live a hundred years yet they have marked the time of the stars so precisely that we stand before them unconched and naked before the magnetic field of time.

His majestic tentacle penetrated the enthralled deep until the black hole shot out its lights.

The words of the poets are spoken in eternity and time is lucky just to echo them.

Where housing is scarce there are lots of mansions.

The rich are a minority we could do without.

They pay them in secret that they might pray in silence.

Human consciousness is attuned to cataclysmic phenomena.

Why should dexterity be confused with science?

Mammon's Priapus rises in Messer's eyes.

Life is made up of thoughts one has never had before.

They are like poaching wolves on the borders of peace.

Is life to be a forsaken experience?

Public opinion is the puppet theater of democracy.

Like original primadorfs they shall come over the sand dunes in their metallic buggies.

He may look like the devil but from his eyes there is a rash of love that could melt a chocolate coffee table.

The media and right wing politicians have put the lid on all forms of social evolution.

Like a blind man he writes of paradise.

Neither an astronomical pig chucker nor a square-footed zit popper be.

Life is immediately predicated by ambient circumstances.

Finding diamonds, he sculpted gold chains to harness them.

Life has its own gravity.

O Teflon penis in velvet vulva bloom.

The visual medium cheapens the currency of ideas.

Mountain silence chilled in ice.

To enjoy art is art itself.

Without stress you tense up.

Noses are aspects of human geography.

An existentialist is someone who feels like an udder.

Adults are children who have become ill.

Some people put out one watt and are praised, others put out one thousand and people put on their shades.

The cure for depression is political activism.

Some people have attitudes others have art etudes.

Time proceeds at such a significant pace that there is no point in pushing it along.

The great Socratic praxis of education is best put forth by great teachers.

Any one who can collect his or her thoughts will in the future find a treasure.

Bull chirping: no bird or bull beefs as much as man of Earth.

You don't have to be smart to love but you have to be dumb not to. Has summer gone so soon to hibernate in Saskatoon?

To form gemniparous artifacts or perish in the penumbra.

She danced she raved she saved she knew she loved she danced she speaks with her eyes twenty languages.

I saw the flash of doom in an amanita muscaria.

The more channels you have open the more music you hear.

The road to heaven seems paved with hell's intentions.

I don't know where the center begins and the middle ends.

It's like traveling at the speed of light, it takes time.

Madness has a golden lining.

We sat on the porch like cats watching fish go by.

He ate not an oeuf and starved.

Trapped like monkeys with their cookies in a jar.

Life is a joke and then you weep.

Schizophrenics like angels in a bell jar smile through hell.

Time was once cheap.

Dialectical materialism was to become sensuous.

Beautiful stones set in burnished dross.

The big book with its pages parted in the middle coifed a four-legged desk.

The cold fries of anger burn in our gut.

Re-tribalise.

Churches are cemeteries for the spiritually dead.

Right wing governments deny justice to the world.

The war which has not ended has yet to come and the war which has yet to come has not ended.

Nothing pushes drugs more than blatant hypocrisy.

It's in the city you lean out the window and sing your own song to the sun-god.

Once and still Christian Russia versus once and still Christian America. Bombs away!

Small business hides behind the skirt of big business.

In one generation we fall into social chaos.

A frogy prince came handsoming along.

A few hundred years only in the land of the grandfathers and I am becoming its mother's son.

Every citizen of every nation shall be truly free and every need of humankind shall be met.

This is a Faustian World where what the devil bets on is a sure thing.

Do birds remember dinosaurs when they see jumbo jets?

This must be the day.

Is the universe going to take this beautiful generation away? On the table the roses are brown.

Gracious that time then as now gives birth to many poets.

A socialist Christian atheist: alive and well and living in reality.

He was a verbalist par excellence and the brother of a herbalist.

The mussels ate the message.

For people such as yourself who for pay have abandoned goodness.

Art is god.

Your desire escaped the velocity of time because it reflected off a past event.

Foraging in the same treasure throve he found only want.

It is easy to preach wisdom from the other bank of the river.

Just as much as one of good hearing is deafened by it, only one who pays no attention dances to the sound of no music.

He asphyxiated on an anal anabolism and was thus thwarted by a rectal thrombosis.

In the city life will go on hydroponically.

A dream event a blessed traumatic event or reality dreamed.

Share the isotopes of consciousness.

You got good glowing going.

In heaven nobody knows who you are but in hell everybody knows.

Bartok is beautiful.

Soon we will have non-polluting cars.

One never takes the hardest path for selfish reasons.

Words are as the polishing of a grain of sand, a work of merit and of thoughtfulness.

Genes are the biological result of physics and chemistry.

Everybody in business, politics, media and even the citizen seems to be committing moral suicide.

They think aloud their awful thoughts.

They are born in the dust of another generation's glory.

Earth love where the heart is placed in a celestial vortex which has a known communality.

Could only madmen stop the madness.

They descend into hell yet appear to rise like gods.

The right is wrong most of the time and the left is right some of the time.

Some facilitate by making difficult.

as women walk behind bamboo…

An isotope of thought is a fiber optic beam.

And what, my head on the eternal pillow, will I then see?

Myself dancing on a few gene turds in a bubble bath of nerds.

Aim for the stars you who grovel on the ground of eternity.

The solution for the pollution is the annihilation of the collusion.

and there is time only to fart and suck limes

Public opinion is like A I D S., people pass it around without knowing they have it.

The turd at the bottom of the pile was the first one laid.

The pig's poop is heaven's dope.

The media is scared of reality.

There is heaven on the tip of any wand.

Memory percolated to the tip of my consciousness.

The world is one giant Aztec victim fire.

Military implications of modern psychology?

For every creature burning in the fire, umpteen millions doused.

A veritable glacial dyspepsia.

Daydreaming in the same posture I enjoyed the smell of burning newspaper.

To see a palm in the hollow of your hand.

Newton was a third of reality.

There has never been a "moral society", therefore we can not strive to create one it is truly hopeless.

We have never had a truly good world but we can strive to create one... it is not hopeless.

Art is polished impulse.

Capitalism is the spiritual sin called the sin of Simon.

Music is intellectual sound.

The double positive which requires no, neither either's nor knows nos.

It's all like daydreaming in acrylics.

Pabulum suckers unite.

Mental health and madness ride the same Mobius strip.

You get caught in the fish net according to your size.

Language being in the ocean of consciousness reveals unconsciousness.

With the Original Sound of creation, the word began flesh.

Language and consciousness married and became god on earth...the only god on earth.

Never jump to conclusions unless you have to.

Politics is the viral outcome of human aggregation.

The unified field of art.

He put the proposition in front of the clause and annulled the conclusion.

And we go into the fry like an army of wimps, crying.

I have seen into the future and dare not say what I saw.

He fell through the floor of his emotional stasis.

Illuminated yet grotesque and imponderable soldiers of a death star.

Escape from numerology.

In today's media, the past is not news.

Even though the solution to human problems is eminently rational, such undertakings must find their praxis in an affectedly conducive manner since the point of the exercise is a sharing of experiences pertinent to our otherwise ineffable condition.

Consciousness is an imperishable project.

Words hold the secrets of time.

Roses in snow banks sweat out the long winter nights.

Humanity is a failure.

Beauty easily transcends an ugly physiognomy.

The free world is caught in the peripatetic nightmare of American politics.

They may all have different answers but the question is always the same.

When we speak do we emit ions of negative positivity or of positive negativity?

He is trying to conceal the pleasure he is experiencing from our praise.

Money is the problem in the equation.

Money devalues life.

Seagulls head far out to sea to find shelter from our awful calm.

Gone forever, here to stay.

Doing nothing with resolve catches fish.

Birds like snowdrops fall on the inland field.

Save the earth, save the air, save the seas, save space, salvage time, save the insects, the creatures, save the humans.

Where is the Oronoco from Bantustan? Dust to ash to grass to dust to ash to grass.

He created a circus mundi for the personae he was minding.

Are his verbal skills derived from his affability or is his affability derived from his verbal skills?

The great dragon with sinuous limbs wraps human nature up into its cosmic shell.

Poetry is the perfume of materiality.

Poetry is beauty made from the muck of pain and joy.

And now they seek mantras in the sky.

Because of art...they do not die.

A voice from long ago harmonizes with the wind.

The rich live off the avails of human misery.

The hippies were Einsteinian.

We give soul to each other.

Thesis or prosthesis?

Our present state of consciousness is a visceral dilemma.

The stars shed their trillionth tear of light upon us.

Pro-sociophobics against nuclear war.

Porky Pig's tail is part of the Egyptian alphabet.

We sit and watch the clockwork of time unwind in our personal reality.

The Emperor and Empress of the land beyond funerals and births have seeded us here for their awesome amusement.

Your humor never ceases to escape me.

One thousand and one American nights.

The tiger is still made of paper.

The Buddha's buddies.

I will be back to be I will as I am as I am as I am that I am I will be back to be.

In the temporality of music the intellect can soar.

She talked algebraically…like an angel.

Blessed for being stomped on?

Devices are the codes of good art.

Self-praise does no one harm.

I sat there in the public lavatory and made a perfect stool of myself.

They will read books by the light of eels and whisper sweet nothings in the light of glowworms.

Newtonian fascists.

Art is heroic.

Paradise is in Hell.

Did Jesus commit suicide?

Art rises from hypocrisy.

They were born again because the first time was not enough.

The hippies were an answer to the promise of time.

To be more precise and fix time for a more particular undertaking.

The hummingbird sings perched on an atom of bliss.

We are in a media state of awareness like fish in a sushi roll.

Torrigo by Carlos Chipotle.

Pass onto me o Buana your perpetual archetypes said Eve to Adam.

A minority in the right cannot easily bind a minority in the wrong but a minority in the wrong can easily bind a minority in the right.

The Universe must truly have been bored to make all this.

B.S. is awesome.

The wisdom gets lost in the message.

Illuminatingly imponderable and grotesque soldiers of a hymn.

Poets walk by the window all day long.

Who knows what times are being considered in the great twilight.

It is no wonder that the western world is in such a mess… since public opinion is the engine of democracy's politics.

The original primadorf is coming in a huge metallic buggy. He is presently bouncing about in remote sand dunes.

The land of no McDonalds.

People often demean themselves when they flatter themselves.

Sulfur the breath of the inevitable as you would sulfur yourselves.

Any one time and everyone time and a hi o silver of a time.

Capitalism is the enslavement of mankind by mankind, socialism is the enslavement of mankind for mankind.

Was christianism a revolution on roman ruins founded?

Clouds like boats in the sea pass by.

Why do the guilty feel so innocent and the innocent feel so guilty? A spinach and caviar samosa with a glass of lambrusco.

Light golden fields of Van Goghian color.

Except for the wicked America is not the land of opportunities.

He was a sheriff's deputy and he filled in all the blanks.

We came out of the sea and beached our human emotions.

To mint a thought is to coin a phrase.

One is totally translucent and has a cubic density, another is a white vapor which has the intensity of time.

Koan: pen scratching on paper mice crunching on rice what mind doing?

To Mao: May the honorable one rest in this shallow earthen grave with the other giants of this globe's hour of glory in the sun.

This is a world filled with dried up mucous membranes.

Hippies will reign supreme at last.

Don't use terminology as an excuse for lack of theory.

Auto-humans of their own mystery made themselves and dreamt with pleasure the dream of history.

Between yin and yan there is a cedilla.

Between yin and yan there is a gorilla.

We need more left-handed things and gizmo.

Often artists are a work of art themselves.

Like cupid strident in hand.

Riding giant coy in an antediluvian age.

The man bore the burden and the woman bore the child of the burden.

God must have been bored when he made us since all he does is play with us.

A lexicon of contemporary forgetfulness.

From Xanadu to Perrier.

Earthling children of mother, man sons and daughters of the perpetual war about and beyond almost everywhere.

Genes are the progeny of the original iota.

Born in the dust of glory.

Earth love where the heart is placed in celestial vortexes which have a special cosmic birth.

Life is not behaving well.

Like an isotope of thought in a fiber optic beam we live to die and die to live.

Our choice is either to give the Earth back to the great One whole and human or to blow it up in Satan's name and his deck of right wing cards.

Life is a high-pitched state of consciousness.

Before we make the Earth like the orbs above all naked of life and light the green fuse's fire thereby remaining ignorant of our mysterious sentience forever.

The world economy is a one town company store.

They walk in their dream state and speak with the semblance of authority and I awake in awakedness answer them " Yahoo" but they cannot hear.

In 1984, 1984 came through.

Self-destruction is the last resort of self-protection.

The matador circumcised his tonsils and began to recite hymns.

Women of the oases in desert dunes dance on troubled waters.

Catacombs made of cobwebs.

Ah! Grande Merde.

A little patience is far better than a stick.

For Americans it is particular to the Tripoli of the situation.

They will soon wrap themselves around our succulence.

The oases in the armpits of sand mountains are awesome.

They say that god is still hanging around but nobody is sure.

Schizophrenia is a mental adjustment to political unreality.

They shall not keep from the hog the hogwash.

I see the world electric a medium and a message.

My mind has crammed itself with the grammar of sin and found guilt everywhere but where it truly belongs in political circles.

They are on public opinion auto- programming.

Force over finesse à la Yankee.

I see a zillion doves with the fig of peace in their beaks hurrying across the face of time.

Words are heaven's real Manna.

How what where when and why not.

The wise catch the passes from the great quarterback.

It used to be that we all ate corn at harvest time and played with each other in the bails of hay.

Before birth and after life there is only one master.

He hangs sadomasochistic paraphernalia from his ceiling.

A world anagogic history.

A psychological charge of energy from the ideogenic concepts of the sages.

Thoughts drawn from the far reaches of mentation.

A sexuality and morality pertinent to the sentience of humans on the planet.

He had no problem flying but his landing was atrocious.

It is all ego-glitz.

Molten metal and moonshine sea at the platinum hour.

Though he came from bimbodom, in his mind he never left the place.

True to the effete and emotive optimist, he was a real pinko deist.

Yet will their bright spirit fly with eagles in the bright morning sky.

You have failed your country and the earth you are not what you seem to be and by your pithy means all is nearly lost.

Lust is my horizon.

He came from some remote hinterland from god knows what bullshit hectares of fervid land.

Choice is the damnation of fools.

Religion and money are supposed to be two different things.

Many stars will turn around before it's your goodnight young man and not so many before it's your goodnight old man.

They lock their thoughts in ice cubes.

All our dancing cannot change reality.

A secret locked in tongues like a bag of truth tightly strung.

He swore with rectum graphic hysteria.

The earth still mystified by its priests struggles for its self-revelation.

A field of horse manure smells better than all this right wing political crap.

With a deep breath we came into this world and with a deep breath we leave it.

His grip on reality was loosened when his bank account was emptied.

The image in their mind suffers from being poorly inspired.

Their mind is an unstamped coin.

These times would not appear so dangerous if images of hell were not so prevalent.

Is tomorrow the next day?

It is timed in time the birth of the magic spasm.

Modern psychological consciousness.

In the membrane of remembrance a kilowatt struggles to make sense.

Happiness is the enjoyment of self-taught and other learned behavior.

There are nations of ideas that must stay unpopulated.

He picked his nose and bourgeoisified all over my face.

To find humanity through our femaleness and our maleness.

Artists don't throw their sands on the shoals of money.

The transaction did not materialize because of the cash flow problem that was on hand.

St. George is now defender of the dragon.

I was fiberglassed at the notion of a plastic nonentity waltzing through eternity nonchalantly.

Poetry is the ability to steal from grammar all of its rules.

We can scale that hill after we attempt this mountain.

The cost of bigotry is hell.

A pyro-plastic lake of ash.

There is a lot of geometry in smoke and mirrors.

Romance is the best sequel to an odious odyssey.

Des gouttes d'eau au fond de l'eau.

The birds, their territories reduced to nothing shriek in fright and apprehension.

I feel as useful as a slide rule in the desert.

In western society we have lost Earth"'s ancient customs.

Aztec sacrifices pale when compared with the horrors perpetrated by European men.

Why put brakes on a flight of fancy?

Practice amorousness.

An increment of good over evil is worth its weight in gold.

Right-wing bible maniacs persecute the children of god from Nicaragua to Ethiopia.

They shall become nations they shall be culminations they shall become nations.

A prearranged agreement that predates the candidacy propelled him to victory.

The most speckled aspect of the spectrum is still unidentified.

Their response to life is premedicated.

Either we have gone mad or we are still at the same place.

Ridicule is an instrument of reality.

I saw god on TV; gray stuff called the human brain.

Fear of nudity is a sin.

Nous avons tous apperçù rien.

The political dementia continues.

The will of Allah is still in eclipse.

If the yellow pages are the bible of free enterprise the white pages must be the new testament.

Today the Sheriff of No-Thingham has Robin Hood by the bag.

The demise of hegemony.

American hegemonistic chauvinism.

Pleasures ripple me.

A world through which the ultimate is interpreted in forms.

He wags his prepuce in the crepuscule hopelessly.

She keeps on solidifying the ephemeral.

I am at issue with the issue.

L'amour sest arrèté au phosphore.

This god is an abstract non-entity who is mad as hell.

The wisdom gets lost in the language.

Eternity and time together as one entity.

Poems are the perfume of mentation.

Ozone O Meo.

Rest homes are orphanages for the elderly.

We have not yet reached the zenith of our apoplexya.

The solution to many of our problems might be found in the San Andréa's Fault.

My desire escapes the velocity of time.

The virtue of the virtuous is Herculean for many but for others it appears Daffy Duckish.

Man; Earth's flailing intelligence.

If your mother and your father do not want you then why would you want to be born?

And what's to be? A world full of dried up mucous membranes?

Share the isotopes of consciousness.

There will come a day when the stolen treasures of conquered peoples will be benevolently returned to their national museums.

From the sacred ball game of the Aztecs to baseball; America's feathered serpent still plays with smoking mirrors.

The Spaniards navigated to Tenochtitlan because their for-originals had migrated there 20 thousand years ago.

There is egg on everyone's face.

Does god have amnesia?

Artistic expression is rare. It reveals itself often at an early age.

It should immediately be bolstered.

Most artists suffer from great neglect. Yet they are the cornerstone of every civilization.

In the future, Christians will need neither priests nor churches.

They thirst for the ephemeral.

If the world is in god's lap, what is he doing with it?

An Einsteinian homologue; liberator of all human energy.

The rich are always with us (to make us poor).

The Earth is a yolk with its yuk eking out of its shell.

In the future we will have Peace Officers instead of Police Officers.

God is responsible for the Devil.

The privatization of social services is undemocratic.

The yards and harrows of belligerent fortunes.

Life becomes death and in the meantime it's a family picnic in a park run by despots.

Nature is substance and form. By transubstantiation (fish eat fish) form (fish) is maintained.

Since WW. Two we have lived in WW. 2 1/2.

Of those of us who are born many are aborted politically.

Older and older, faster and faster, sooner and sooner, longer and longer.

It is amazing how some people treat other people as if they were human beings.

The mentality of man was monumental when Claudius Claudianus expressed the breasts of the Deities.

The phone's cord curled like a cat's tail down the TV screen and waved off reality from the face of my daydreaming.

It was you who first made me hungry and sick who now feed me and heal me.

A blessed traumatic event, a dream event.

Allegory, grandiose imagery, fecundity of sound ischemic seizures...

paralysis of feeling... mind.

It never stops and I never cease to despair.

There is evidence of new-century-consciousness.

Gezerb gazeeb ganad zub za.

Agapornis roseicollis.

I tell you old people take a devil with you and drop him off in hell on your way to paradise.

He reads the words off the TelePrompTer whether they are lies or truths.

They incite the majority against the minorities so that they might profit by this discord.

The Being who is responsible for me is responsible lock stock and barrel.

Inter-convoluted thought forms.

With his children, a father salts the seas of destiny.

Make the linguistic chronology grammatically coherent.

It amazes me to remember so clearly that I have forgotten something just now.

After the party only the ones who drank nothing walked away drunkenly.

Faith has not played its hand and destiny is not dined out.

The gods have not kept their drugs from us nor their wisdom good or bad ...they know we are as they are.

For some the downside is the upside.

1 trillion Buddhas on their thrones float above us: nest-ce-pas, nest-ce-pas, nest-ce-pas

You can save the Earth by a Love meditation if the alpha waves don't reveal your location to the force that evil men and women are tapped into.

Bach was a Newtonian composer.

Politicians are batting zero percent in a dark dome.

On the tombstone of this once promising century write, ""Here lie the warmongers, the haters who outlawed love.""

Hate is eased because love is so hard to communicate.

The fact of right wing politics is war, death, tragedy, poverty, economic chaos and social dysfunction of all kind. A plethora of evil perpetrated by political wrongdoers.

Abraham? Moses? Jesus? Freud? Marx? Einstein?

It will be an unknown pity when this brain perishes having toiled in the forbidden valley and found most of the fruits and flowers therein at the foot of the only good.

I have seen into the future and it is here now.

Lawlessness at the top is worse than lawlessness at the bottom.

Totley Humbug, word addict.

The great One made the elephant strong so that he can shake delicious acacia pods out of a tree.

You can't blow without cheeks.

As if stuck in a hologram old notions hold themselves forth in space like the icons of a bygone era.

The bubbles pool in time's quicksand.

Law is a cheese work of loopholes.

Good fighting evil causes less death, suffering and destruction than doe's evil un-opposed.

Ye gad ye bushes and ye stolid things, you orics and fricassees of nonsense you stool headed men of bones.

Strong thoughts Picassoed his facial expressions.

The race to heaven is thwarted by politics.

The bottom line belongs to the bottom.

It all started a long time ago and nobody knows why.

Let the politicians and business men who make us hate...beware.

The mental prolusions sinistered in the perfume redolated in the levodexterousness.

Lunch; spinach and caviar samosa and blush wine.

I know you from the land of my eternity.

The debased cosmology of human consciousness will prove equal to the heights of thought's tomorrows. He who lays the corner stone is then cursed by everyone

Egoglitz.

There is a plethora of things left to define...and

in the mind of man still a mishmash of impenetrable mysteries.

They stand up on their toes and rooster their anger.

Even Hell must be better than this pseudo-paradise.

The plague of blackened sunlight promised.

Leftest deftest light.

Orgasmo Xamphyr; playboy seraphim.

Poverty really fills the silence in this country;

It is a pity that the mirror at the end of the optics of your eye is blank.

The Earth is a hologram.

The offices, the jails, institutes and streets are filled with the unhappy peoples of the Americas.

Media's lurid holiday from the starving children and their broken families has lasted long enough.

The media is a Big Lie pusher.

And it was told that the bevy manacled to the zoo's bars harped on and on, with shining hinds unprospering behind.

On the west coast you emote with the flora and on the east coast you emote with the Rasa.

Psycho-Mortadella.

But for previous slaughters we would be eating McWhale burgers.

Where was else needed but thought writing mind in being.

Time to seal the seal, to end the times, to facilitate the first of a newly born real.

Hypocrisy works.

He found himself amongst the sat-jupons.

Only one war left and only one peace left.

Is not memory a time travel machine?

I was educated by abysmally ignorant people, and subjected to an abysmally ignorant cause that keeps on reproducing itself.

The Love of the Life Spirit, the Love of the Whale, the Love of the Dolphin, the Love of the Mastodon, the Love, the Human Love...

I saw the holograms of the great One's grammar in the nimbus of light.

Gravity is god's and god is gravity.

Clouds steam in the heavens...the human rice.

You can still fling a curtain above its rod.

They launch out of their eyes pyroplastic looks.

The US. wants to put a necklace of bombs around the Earth's deep space.

Life is not a game of chess but chess is a game of life.

I'll wear my holy tempest shoes down by the riverside, down by the riverside.

I'll wear my holy tempest shoes, till the Day been by. Who has turned my wine to water and my bread to dust?

It took but a moment for me to revert to the acrimony of time as space stood still and proved itself pervious to everything.

The old rabbit knows finally that the carrot is attached to its head.

Our new priests are broadcasters.

We are all intricately politically manipulated.

A fierce thing in the heart, a strong shooting out of a lost rib in the zone an incensing of consciousness.

Sweet, sweet music heaven, heaven, heaven.

A new prayer: forgive me o my planet my selfish sins though they burn holes in the atmosphere.

A new commandment; No tree shall thou cut.

O Heavenly beings, help this planet in this hour of need.

No more private-interest only media. The community must take back the airwaves.

The private sector has stolen the people's pharmacopoeia.

Lost daydreaming in a car mirror.

Old hens squawk at the sight of young cocks cuckolding in the barnyard.

He wanted her to splurge all her pre-mucals, instead with a gleaming smile she hyphenated an epithet.

Could an inarticulate ultra mundane intelligence have conceived and effected through Judaism, Christianity and Islam thousands of years of fiery conflict?

Their wisdom shows in the fabric of their smile.

The eyes and the mind spend most of the time fooling themselves.

At the risk of being sure of offending; the Universe is just a Big Crap God took once upon a time.

First you are born then you spend your whole life apologizing.

Anyone who keeps too close to this or that side of the law infuriates the law.

There must be a connection between the egg and the ego since they both bear a living thing.

To have stolen the Earth's bounty from so many children past, present and future makes human nature inexplicable.

I was dreaming in empty space when I saw Baba Ramdas roller skating on an ice-rink.

What in the depth of Earth's seas so frightened us that we scrambled madly onto Land?

Children are maxi lingual univerbs.

Partisan politics have added one more layer of conflict to that of sectarianism religion, custom and creed.

Why is the cream at the bottom of the jar?

Why does evil and confusion stand before us preaching? Art is an act of faith always beyond the reach of the artist. Jesus dammed social sin but forgave personal sin. Paradise begins and ends with $E=Mc^2$ I shall lift my shoes to heaven.

The distance between Time and Eternity is $E=Mc^2$

Contrary to the oft-stated aphorism, genius is often found in a nutshell.

I believe in the reconciliation of all humanity.

Businessmen are too greedy to understand the dignity of peoples and nations.

Nobody really owns anything it is really just all air bubbles.

Our dreams being too short lived, it is necessary to wake up.

Life can be tough when you are a bozo.

Words hold the secret of life.

Capitalism is sometimes like social thalidomide.

An arch criminal is destroying the creator's work.

Some people suffer from a pronounced infarction of their nitty gritty.

There is always somebody whose looks or mind can sauce up nature.

The mollusks of life slimed on and on.

Blessed is the downpour of rain all over the Earth.

For the poor it is bread and water for the rich it is croissants and Perrier.

Without love we are just furniture.

Oh, when the heart breaks loose from its dams.

Don't worry about it, he said: I would only take you to court if it was cheap and a lot of fun."

If we knew that we were not going to be employed we could decide not to be born.

Intellectual anecdotes of short duration.

The 80"s have been a righting political orgy.

It is the genius of memory to be imperfect.

It seems that the only antidote to the human condition is death.

The stones of thought skip on the surface of consciousness and plunge into the unconscious like a meteor in the night.

Without affect the mind is defective.

Truly the Earth is the devil's paradise.

Life lives even at the very borders of the absolute.

I saw the native ancestors standing behind every tree.

Memory is triggered by instances which dupe all.

Oh, those egregious fantasies.

I groaned to think of her labial pallor.

Let the shoe wear the right foot.

What assertions are associated with asininity?

It is calypso time in the memory cells.

I may not know the way to heaven but the way to heaven knows me.

Monsters are throwing existence into hysterical convulsions.

Our jails are filled with native people and white Indians.

I rise like mineral water in the morning in a state of ebullition from the deep wells of sulfurous motion within me.

The cedar liquid perfume of paradise.

Adolescence is being dynamited out of the waters of childhood.

I see in a former metempsychosis, galaxies of snow.

Politics un-catholicked me.

The heart is born aloft on musical phrasings.

I sat Buddha Eyed and grinned sadly at the missing Madonnas and the lifeless E Pluribus Unum.

Human neurons function at the speed of light.

Continue thus you madmen and soon we will begin the countdown of days

It may be a play on words but it sure looks like a game of chess.

Bullshit was a monumental task for him.

It was trippy and what I just said bounced off the walls of thought and forming a globule vanished in a spatial trilogram.

A worm through a lawnmower will go 10 meters in five sections.

I was a Peekfreen freak in a cookie store.

Totemic upon the wall the image of my imagination stood forthright and tri-dimensional arching with the reflection of my original thought.

The ultimate majesty of nature in all its mucous ness.

What is more whale like than human intelligence?

No man is an island…but I sure feel like one.

Life is so bad sometimes that one feels like jumping of one's tricycle.

Bullshit travels faster than truth.

I often feel like an iota in a punctum.

If it weren't for the staff mental institutions would be great.

Beyond light no end in sight.

Did the Great One place a halo around Saturn to prove to cynical men that He/She can put a halo about their head?

Today's political class is the stuff of holocaust.

The media is sometimes a cull-de sac.

Violets like marmosets peek through the wild gloom.

Our human sea-past; when shall it be restored to memory?

Private ownership of the means of public communication is undemocratic.

Let's get everything ready and put it on pause.

What can the people do with messengers who act as if they Are the message?

God is the Egg the chicken came after.

I sense an incessant stream of instantaneous commands.

Kids: the planetary zits of Homo habiles.

Maniacally depressed Canadians look forward to an age of Tory darkness.

The right peeks euphoric over the fence of social justice to rally to the long term goal of a republican North America...and cowards...cowards everywhere...and no true soul in sight.

This society has not lived up to this century's expectations.

How dare we send the R C M P. to raid native villages.

Make bold...sound the alarum...the right wing monster prances before us.

Des chimères rien que des chimères.

Although the Word is mankind's most sacred trust it is also its most defiled.

The 60"s cultural revolution proposed an agenda of world peace, world justice and worldwide responsibility for the Earth. But the reactionaries mounted a contra-agenda and these last three decades have fallen into the pit of their monstrous sorcery.

Some are Golfarbians and believe in the entrails of poles others see Golfarbians eating steak.

And saw drakes nesting in a pond...

Trans-stellar sperm.

We are crunched by the machinery of time and pinned like insects to gravity how to escape?

Gold is best used for art and for arthritis.

Some put money in the stock market others in the stock market and many in both.

National sacrifice zones where the great crimes of industry can hide in medieval quicksand and hellish bogs where once the awesome graces of creation grew.

Upon Apollo's troubled brow hung Conan the American his lips twisted in a wry grin.

The Poor's fractured imagination cannot find comfort in indignation.

To soar above and in the midst of clouds both rural and sublime.

Time hardens even the softest soul.

In the Original Medium the Chicken and the Egg are in one Rooster.

Earth the unfinished star.

If the mind cannot awaken from this bad dream then only the heart can.

The news does not exist.

Blood is a chemo-electric set of rules.

Go swift thought and widen the horizon of whites.

In the ""great freedom loving"" country of America Benjamin Spock was arrested at a peaceful rally protesting homelessness.

The truth is given very little airtime.

Right-wing propagandists fill the public's media.

Why does free speech so often result in selling sex and beer?

A dance: their legs changed hips in a clashing of limbs wrapped in acrylic clouds.

Hummingbirds love flowers: their bellies full, they sweat in the morass of summers breathing in a glorious solar holocaust.

The Earth's New Jerusalem, the stellar mea culpa, the paranoid phoenix, the spatial gem.

Reality does not hide from lunatics.

The cosmic script is hard to read.

Since everything implies a question then speaking should imply an answer.

Ah! The eternal dreaming of the psychic corpus.

A center for the remembrance of assumptions.

Lots of tendentious tentacles were slimed out.

It seems impossible but we can make Earth into Heaven.

A fatted calf am I, nursed by pragmatic reality to find sustenance midst dreams and accept to walk amongst dreamers an inch away from paradise.

We shall empty the Vatican of mundane treasures, the Madonna of Andrew Melon we shall return to Alba. The Sacred rituals of nations we shall return to them and it that now walks freely amongst us will be rendered powerless.

Amazing how music spines itself in space and time.

Canada was a small pocket of sanity in a world thoroughly gone mad but the cloud of native spirits moaning over the desecration of their homeland has lifted the veil of such conceit.

I wonder if the water I put in a tray hours ago has frozen into a cube and why should anyone bother with the useless gratification which imperils the Earth and all its newborn chicks?

The desire to bear children may appear to some to originate from lust

but it is really from the ineluctable drive of the universal creative force.

A friend's acquiescence can restore one's faith one billion percent.

Public places are the parks of humankind's heaven on Earth, and where Buddha and Jesus once preached goodwill.

We have seen the richest bums with the great pedigrees ruin our lives while those without languish in the wisdom once promised onto all.

Chakra Ya!

Who has cut off from us the places where we can rest our head?

Prodigious humanity quelled by the venal lust for green paper.

Come before me in my sleep you who starve five hundred million children that I may create a hell for you similar to the one I have seen on one of the Eternal Continents when I walked with the poet Dante.

Of this world's shadow's light within a breath of casting beams into man's plighted mind but for what thin partition between beast and man.

In pleasure of shared intelligence in a dance of wisdom at her moment reigning.

Loublie se réveil.

The spermatozoa transit distance in the liquidity of time arrested only by the impediment of their velocity.

We go to sleep fully imagining and wake up totally innocent. We forget our dreams. We wake up shattered and piece by piece we must Tai Chi ourselves together again.

Poets chase after images and wind up with rainbows.

Snotso the clown was snotso funny.

They suck out proteins and elucidate hallucinogenic properties.

Satie sweet supple and elastic Satie.

Invite me to that Druidical ceremony and let me strike with pen capitalist and socialist bourgeoisie in the name of one Celestial Community.

Here are we, between our quaking and our becoming.

And we fell into being as seeds from the ideogenic tears of the stars.

The mute hemisphere of the brain is ventriloquist to the other.

Go winged Inuit from ice flow to ice flow, plot your course on that checkerboard of snow and find that sea lion who remembers the First Day of Creation.

When life is pushed to live its ultimate bounds it will find madness so mixed with reality that only the width of its body will keep its feet on Earth.

Music is a play of sound written by the stars for the amusement of awesome beings.

Christian religion has hidden god in black robes, fake ceremonies and hideous moralities.

I choked in my spasms as my youth flickered in the flames of the economic fire and lost itself in artificial heavens.

Their wisdom shows in the fabric of their smiles.

The god of no-choice is an angry static god.

People who demand the death penalty are mostly right wing Christians; curious that God had put a mark on Cain's forehead so that no one should kill him for murdering his brother.

That is the dichotomy between energy and experience. When you have energy you have no experience and when you have experience you have no energy.

Revel's piano concerto in G.

We are squirrels in a cage and a gun is pointed at our head.

Lost Angeles Lost Angeles Lost Angeles.

La démocratie est acheté avec I 'argent des peauvres.

When the artist is dead the work rejoices.

Missing in action of mind, bliss from the voices of women.

Once the New Indians smoked the Peace Pipe, the Great Peace Began. A sign was given out again…the source of understanding sprang up from history's dry well.

The entire content of material thought has for a purpose its own progenitor.

Tax avoiders are the enemies of children and the poor, the homeless, the sick and themselves.

Time cannot deal with itself.

He swooned in a Proustian eternity.

I have probed a hornet's nest and tasted the sweet flower of oblivion but the nightingale still sorrows as she flies over the open field.

He proposed an enthusiastic encapsulation of the dilemma.

Her elucidation was lovely as she reminded us of the archetype.

May the universal illusion experience Samadhi.

Moses died in Greenwich village NY 1961 of arthritis.

Man, who has twice found fire is in legend to return the painful duality of the human condition with the discovery of a third fire.

Society suffers from wisdom phobia.

The intimacy between art and religion reveals the two forces that work upon history.

I was fallen like all but you lifted me up. I fell again and again, again and again thank you.

The first clay tablets were stored in a library in China 4000 years ago.

Once the original impetus is devised the rest is easy.

Fortuitous religious intolerance causing wholesale persecution must be attributed to the exceeding long-suffering of Allah.

The native fathers and mothers are the descendants of the gods of the Americas.

Who cares what your hands are doing when your mind is grooving.

Any rationalization for our individual isolation is immoral.

Men kill in wars they say are justified women have abortions which they say are justified. Only the great One can judge this.

Every society on Earth is a failure.

Where is Kr!!sna? Why omit Brahma? Why forsake Arjuna? Oh, where is the dharma of the Bodhisattvas.

The scandalous and the salacious fly from the green tongue like money from a cash machine.

Those were windowpane days of dreaming in a berserk daze gleaning insights into eternity.

Those stifling halls of glory, in business, politics or academe, where yogis and lingams parade medusa like before the Lagoon of fame.

Economic mercenaries wage war against us.

A plethora of ponderous thoughts.

Clusters of sentient teen-age beings mushroom here and there. Nothing but the adrenaline of youth can save the wild blue yonder.

The children will only know by the seminal vesicles what the truth of life is.

He threw a twenty dollar word at them and when they tumbled for the coins he disappeared.

Mega Cosmic.

Just the continuing saga of one Buddha's incarnation in sentience.

Everything is far more than anyone can bear at one time anyway.

All is art there is no non-art.

Schizophrenics have either heard or seen the great One or the Devil or are affected by either or both of their rays.

Because we are reptilians our mores are reptilian.

He needed a room full of mirrors to take stock of his assets.

To knit the emotional context of happiness in a lifestyle continuum.

He lives like a clean swine in an immaculate garden.

Heterosexual, bisexual, homosexual we are all amoebas with a Mendelianpredicated sexual chemistry.

People who are in the full liberty of their self-expression are beautiful.

Before the chicken and the egg came the rooster.

The sayings of a non-itinerant truant.

The magic of attraction creates a dreamscape.

Sexual intimacy is a learned process.

He stroked the wheel and progeny came fourth.

The media should be scared of itself.

Adults thieve on the childhood of modern generations.

Good means justify a good end.

Emotionally adventuresome, he was sporadically mellifluous.

Let us believe in one universal humanity, neither rich nor poor. Let those who object stay rich on a paradise island far from humanity. Since the only measure of their wealth is the rest of us, let's see how they would enjoy a small world solely for the rich.

Although life is mind, mind is flesh.

The currency of reality is speech.

Our sight ways are polluted with telephone lines.

The New Children are showing us the road to peace.

We will empower ourselves and take back the earth.

T.V. is fiction, an illusion inside the illusion of reality, a surrogate, an escape provided us by those who make us run.

Beautifully Satanic the Angels live in Heaven and Hell.

I saw all the doors of leftist heaven closed.

To give a generation living in the midst of hell a remembrance of eternal hope.

Et des quenouilles et des jonquilles dans un étang se penchent vers le soleil comme des Musulmans.

Fatherless and fodder less in America.

Democracy is hell, capitalism is hell, aristocracy is hell, communism is hell. Culture is heaven art is heaven mores are heaven is heaven and hell is hell. Heaven is hell and hell is heaven.

Reality is a divine elixir, an ultra mundane experience.

Emotional beauty is the loveliest.

One more transcendental conniption.

You can keep me poor and you can keep me blessed but who are you to say how poor or how blessed I should be.

She or he who diapers a joy as it flies lives in eternity's sunrise.

Birds drank from the tears which ran into my mouth as I stood there frozen in a state of ecstasy.

Crying is just another way of sweating.

My mind saturated with feelings filled my ears with a high-pitched ring.

She threw ideas to the ground and made all Earths big with life.

Still there are no democracies only self-serving delusions pushed by those who grease the wheels of greed.

We sleep and we wake and still we sleep, only some awaken beyond these two these are demons or gods they sleep; they wake and still they sleep only one is never asleep and never awake in any case the poets are right 'tis but a dream a dream of sleep and awakening.

The game of love is not for wimps.

Our heroes have bad reputations in the media: environmentalists, peaceniks, left-wingers, liberals, teachers etc.

What is the matter on Earth or what on Earth's the matter.

A glasnost of the psychological sciences is in the offing.

People are history gods and politicians are the tale.

Des tas de merde tous.

Was Shakespeare French? Was his name Robert Branle-Lance.

I lived on islands wild where herons shit on cow-pissed swamps by the sea.

Generations arise to free reality now laden with shackles.

The secrets of the State are written on the faces of the children.

Media hides in money's skirt while our children die of cancer caused by chemicals in their food.

Rimbaud, Picasso, Ravel, Giacometti.

Tired of choking on his own spasm he fought with the very same wits.

Artists should radicalize people for the sake of society.

We shall sea.

The media cartel.

Can a mere pawn capture a king.

The sorted screws bolt the scene.

Beauty is in the eyes of a Beethoven.

The Velcro creeks on the leather sofa.

Life is a Gas.

Is this Moscow or Washington?

You can gape and fart at the world all you want but it won't change much.

Never eat a croissant in bed.

What diaphanous lingam laid out the lotus and the magnolia.

The natives of America are in a Diaspora.

What would pigs on an iceberg eat?

There is nothing wrong with materialism as long as it is used for humane purposes.

A seating of fat cats at a feast meant for gods and not for beasts.

Our media...parrots in a box.

An insult is better than a cheap compliment.

I saw a lonely man dancing whilst holding a magnifying glass to his arm and asked him why. He said he was dancing with someone very small.

Does x plus minus equal y minus plus?

The vaporization of interlocking relationships due to the economic agenda is reducing humanity to a cyclical and downward spiraling vortex that leads to oblivion.

Humanity is so busy making money that it forgets to make humanity.

With eyes blazing with erratic visions a mind swelled with infinity and imploded like a black star.

The prolific destinies of perverted powers!

I am the only me that lives and I only live with myself.

The one good thing about god is that he gave us a mind to fuck around with.

Political criminals luxuriate in their own largesse.

The old testament belongs to Pinochet but the new testament belongs to Gandhi.

The vowels were all that remained after I finagled his brain.

Conservative politicians have made their awful delusions our reality.

Has the magic of the Earth disappeared.

Half a century since Kermit dropped Einstein's equation on Japan.

The world goes round and round but there is a heavy cam on it.

Believe it or not I have seen angels even in a bar.

And now for the major part of a while.

Newspapers de priorise the truth.

La réalité m'épine trop avec son grand caractère.

I hate laughing at things I don't understand.

Our cars are urban camels in the desert of oil-based capitalism.

Outchies are ego sensitive persons.

The fools emoted like Romulans.

It was luck at first sight.

Politics in the US. is a mystery even for the sophisticated.

The media rules the mental waves.

He was satiated with a slumber sandwich.

Inflation is here only to keep pace with inflation.

Un monde cocufié par les syllabes.

It was a blessing in this guise.

All of consciousness is language.

Johnny Barbarian.

Oil Power Ego.

Psycho-isolation can result in anxiety attacks.

Canada suffers from Culturephrenia.

It is as good for me to love for a moment than not to love at all.

Our eyes and lips sunk into the nebulous flesh of our sweet young skin.

An excratorium.

Can America live in a humane world?

Time is shortening Apocalyptically.

Kill that noise and bomb the shit out of that trash is an American dictum.

Prokofief; sonata for clarinet and piano.

An airplane of thoughts.

You are born into stress to die into stress, meanwhile alliaceous forces pump your bloodstream until you evaporate in your dreams.

I can wake up only in one dream.

Behold the fabled riches of Arabia.

And away we go she said as we put on her coat.

It was a large exaggeration.

Once upon a time there were no automobiles.

The character is in the parameter of the personality in its natural flux or fluxes and is within these parameters to express personality which expresses character.

Political gangrene corrupts the body politic and limits democracy.

The hum of reality sounds like "Aoum» or Om" from far away or deep inside.

The hum of reality's electric hinges ohm's through hell.

Il y avait un flou entre moi et le réel.

Your hand is blood vessel city.

From Udaipur to Aurangabad

The guy is so great he is not fit to tie his own shoestrings.

The gorgeousness of mind stuff.

The world in a nutshell: fat sugar salt and alcohol.

Daddy make big bucks…children perish.

I did not read ""The Power of Positive Thinking"" because I didn't think it would do me any good.

It looks like sugar coating but it is like penurysation.

Save the planet: feed a bird in winter.

He was as gentle as a snowdrop on a rose petal.

Santa Claus is a materialist Buddha.

The words were waxed in stone.

Being beauty to bring in the wondrousness, having guile to draw in the lost, and presence to bring in the present being in being.

This wolf dances tonight.

Dream-thoughts my old dream-thoughts have become the future of these times and of recent times past. I was sleeping wide awake in a maelstrom of dreams I remember those visions which have yet to come fortunately I still do not know the time and the place.

The only thing that is keeping him alive is the idea of suicide.

As soon as war begins all of freedom dies.

Being alive is the only thing that is keeping him from committing suicide.

A broken hand does not tell time.

Where iguanas eat exotic flowers the end of dreams begins.

Wars have sucked the virtue of humankind right down to our very marrow yet we elect leaders hell-bent to save false prides at the cost of children's lives.

The great One is all the stars together.

The difference between rumors and truth is research.

Champagne is the equalizer.

If you cannot trust your insights you are worthless.

They said forget the past but I couldn't, instead I saw the past become worse and worse.

Le moulin và trop vite.

The dead shall awaken the dead.

The sands of paradise are filled with tears.

International egotism.

Will the plasmodium dreamer awake?

A Mess Age.

Often, too often the truth is taken for a lie.

What nation on Earth is safe from Uncle Sam.

There is no duty there is only moral apprehension.

Dictatorship over there is dictatorship over here.

A few days in eternity according to Newton Time.

I put my in-breath back into the wisdom.

He was a candy coated devil just like the ones who came before and after him.

News truth: Jan. 22, 1991, BC. a radio station bans John Lennon's song "Give Peace a Chance."

This is no hollow shell. It is an overloaded vessel in a stormy sea.

My vulnerability hardens me.

Those who starve to death fill hell's stomach.

Invoke the universal interest and the individual interest together.

R N A. and D N A. is a spiral staircase between heaven and hell.

Does the Great One shop on Sunday and the Sabbath now?

I wash the petals of a million buds with my tears.

Emotionalize instead of intellectualize.

Hug, caress, expand, touch, emote, feel, realize, suck up, be human.

Oh, the pain in my heart and mind as war begins in history's ancient sands.

History is an Everest of human failure.

Evil will collapse upon itself.

Everybody is crying.

Children's consciousness is full of great vistas.

It is a question of sacrificing my heart to the great pain of life. The great brain is happy the great brain is coming. Argh! In the name of god give to non-religious charity.

Quel Mal.

America will pay the price of its ignominiousness.

The Earth belongs to Heaven but the humans crawling in it have an unknown destiny.

She cried and her tears fell on my body everywhere.

Joseph Lovetongue.

Songs stories things thoughts consciousness dreamlife reality.

Never corner yourself into a box.

Without windows painful darkness.

How many last dawns left inside the immense pale.

Reality is excellent.

Joseph Elephant.

Early bad news is better than late bad news.

Be dynamically honest and true.

He was just recently glued back together.

Planetary gratification.

Il ne faux pas courir la dedans avec des bottes.

My friend went Van Gogh on me.

A problem is half resolved just by dealing with it. Learn to recognize the signal lights of anger and stop.

Do not dislocate your spinal architecture by holding your head up with the palm of your hand.

The fossilized arrogance of the judiciary on Native issues must be exposed.

Monsieur Mitterrand devrait vendre des marons chaud.

The US. is Tyrannosaurus Rex.

If Canada is a multicultural country somebody forgot to tell the media.

Like poetry for morons war correspondents can only talk about the general's stars.

War stops art and there is no life sans art.

A mountain of bits.

That is This.

There will be a day of opening up the green curtain and a sigh will burst forth because an oppressor has been overcome.

Generals are at the bottom of the brain chain.

Right-wing politicians are felons in silk pants.

We must humanize our politics.

An arrogant man takes his ignorance for a divine right.

Do not be afraid of time it takes care of itself.

To beget bejeweled becomings.

The sun the moon and the stars are the anodes and cathodes of our cinematographic consciousness.

Cogito ergo tengo soma.

You can only stretch people's imagination to a certain extent.

Until you learn the valor of loosing as a winner you will always be a bum.

Art subsidizes business.

We live every one of us in the ghost of our projected being.

A live rain deer lives in a stall only for a moment.

That man has speech speaks of nature that it is intelligible speaks of the great One.

The great One has shown his face to precious few.

The beast has entered Jerusalem.

My mind my mind he yelled out in the quiet of his thoughts.

I saw a man who was so smart he did not know what he was doing.

Creation is perishable but the means of creation are imperishable.

Because I am not a politician I have a right to imagine things.

Always try the impossible even though it never works.

Sometimes good ideas are very bad.

Joseph Random.

A maiko dressed like a butterfly flew in the midst of history taking pollen from traditional flowers.

There is a tautology in the cosmology.

What happened? Why is it that most humans cannot speak from their heart with the participation of their mind?

Less than 30000 days O Earth Born!

That we are a plague is too much of a surmise.

The god done it.

Shameless bureaucracies everywhere.

What will this planet do to us?

To try to do everything at once is human and to do it well is godlike.

There are many problems which are resolved by doing nothing but they only work in the context of nothing being organized a priori.

Sounds in the silence like pebbles in a well.

!991 Christians bomb Babylon into Eternity.

I dedicate this to those who know humanity and have no money and not to those who have money and do not know humanity.

The plight of things on Earth.

We cannot find our wisdom thus our world is perishing.

His heart is bigger than his pants.

Rich people should go to poor people's parties.

The audio-visual waves are silent as if dead as the truth is a casualty of self-censorship.

There are flaws in the law and there are laws in the flaws.

What dynamics between Neptune and Uranus.

These times are a vastly staged conspiracy to defraud the planet of its goods and humanity of its entitlements.

When cows are dumb man is dumb because cows without men are as bright as the noonday sun.

And here we are making children for a world so dangerous that it makes Machiavelli look like a wimp in a kindergarten.

Bereft and barren are billions to die like beasts petrified in a last holocaust.

The people the people the people.

May the extraordinary power forgive me for crushing an ant.

We are completely irrelevant.

There is not only a historical, a poetic or a symbolic mythology there is a political mythology.

There is nothing democratic about democracy.

Poetry is madness made relevant.

Poetry is madness made pure.

The Earth in springtime smells spermy.

Is there a solar psychology? Does biological life occur because the magnetic fields of curbed space announce a viable biosphere?

The secret of life is a fast lip.

One trillion camels run over the sands of time in a race started before the time of the giants.

B silent B 4 BS.

What gladness furjoys in the summer wilds somewhat more than star thanked heavens?

The great One put a smile on my face which only the devil can take away.

There is no manna in hell.

Mike Rocosm.

It is might over reality.

The churches censure natural human eroticism.

Reality is a scream.

The media create public opinion and pollsters check how successful they are.

The truth is evident, it is a question of stating it.

Morons reproduce at a high rate of success.

It was easy but you know how hard easy gets.

Thank god that I even I dream of you.

When voting becomes revolting revolution is at hand.

God is great...our children shall be peacemakers.

The rewards of thoughtfulness are greater than the riches of all America.

Pseudo-sexual.

The present sees the future as greater than its past yet the past is greater than the future.

The ideated dreamology of human hubris.

Has god the lord lost and is Earth not the residence of all evil incorporated in mankind.

Reality has to deal with reality.

Reality is the daughter of a virgin father.

R I P: Money.

She chipped out a Nautilus from a chunk of rock and there preserved before her eyes, a ship that sailed the seventh sea.

Nyetworking.

Let us not get upset over forgone conclusions.

Après le révisionism.la révolution.

Journalists should ask: really who, really where, really when, really why, really how.

Transcendence is the rule in heaven.

Our children are at the bottom of this pile of insanity.

Le monde cest une bagatelle.

The politician went on a diet and his psyche disappeared in a forethought.

A Jesus coin.

Let us make the unbelievable believable.

Silent bracken.

Please consult your political horror scope.

Mankind is fertilizer.

LHomme cest de lengrais.

The children are in the midst of our political desolation.

Her flowers smelled all week.

Life is a big party.

If their right wing faith will give them a job or protect them they will proclaim it but if it denies them such they will be silent.

Literature, an unending journey into mega-spasms.

It was a great idea but the execution was terrible.

The annals of Time have taken a strike vote.

Mankind's real enemy is anger.

Falling in love is like jumping off a cliff without a parachute.

You stick the little wick of your mind into the spleen of life.

Playing is a reality activity.

Either he changes the story to suit himself or he changes himself to suit the story.

Reality is pre-recorded.

You mesmerize me, now I will mesmerize you.

Capitalist democracies have checks and balances.

It is the ultimate wrong to make money off creation.

He was a rictus driven wimp after all.

Archetype is a great 21'''st century word.

Butterflies are flying flowers.

Secular humanists are god's true humans.

Art is the religion of secular humanism.

TV is fiction made real.

Delusion is the church of fools.

Schools are Blakean factories for clipping wings.

The artist is the consciousness of the collective unconsciousness.

Speaking is the medium.

With a mystique beyond the cleverness of being he stood lifeful his words.

When priests take money in the name of furthering god's work god becomes a banker and money becomes god.

Human respect first democracy after.

They think they can read other peoples mind but they can't read their own.

The wage-poor waitress took table scraps home to feed her children.

Des bateaux incroyables.

The house of god is built on a pile of manure.

Although contemporary American history disproves it, the American constitution is based on the wisdom of others.

The play cannot be written because of the press of time.

They could not fathom his thinking so they buried him in the pit of their mind.

Reality does not jive.

Lhistoire is social sarcasm of the worst kind.

History is money's whore.

I am too busy doing nothing to do anything.

Tiger tiger burning smugly in the fungus of the night.

The great One is mighty yet we don't live by the rules.

Lhistoire est finit.

The role of being irrelevant is not irrelevant.

We are the plastic generation, we buy plastic with plastic.

I dream not of past darkness but of today's.

The well-being of some is taken from the well beingness of many others.

Echoes in my thought-chamber search for the original thought.

We are like cockroaches in an infected being, if the being becomes healthy the roaches will die.

The gem is rough the jewel is not perfected.

La vie est belle même pour les misérables.

Today even if you win you loose.

The legislative assemblies legislate for fat cats who are destroying our communities and our planet.

Art is an allergic reaction to life.

Hippies painted words and farts in paisley colored forms.

Art pours out of being alive in a strange land.

The closer art expresses in time and space the vital functions of consciousness the stronger the art.

So many tongues species less.

Our greatest duty is in general and in particular to mankind.

Here is the 21"st century a harvest of words.

Only words can heal the world.

I donned my epaulettes and strutted out into the world's vanity.

When you crucify a gentle soul you liberate a devil. When you restrain an artist you imprison the world.

The whole human world will come at once.

It took hundreds of millions of years before humankind invented sunglasses.

The universe is accident-prone.

Something beyond the itch of kind has proven true.

the mirror shows everything but the beholder sees only one thing.

Something is in its being as the thing of things. An entity from all the abstractions present an allness from the unspoken fabric of all immanence.

Earth Flag.

They live off the slaughter of trees so ancient that Angels once sat on their branches.

I see in the faces of the Native peoples of the Americas that we have shamed god.

If the spirit is imagination and the flesh is reality then we are ghosts and the Earth is already in Heaven.

The animals die before our eyes and in our hedonism we do not see the sign of our own forthcoming dying.

I climax to think of human beings behaving in the manner of lovers conscious of the cosmic plan.

The ducks float up and down the ripples as if they rode Cadillacs.

Beauty wins the day.

And here the queen upon a penny lies meaningless except as a symbol of centuries of raping and plundering the continents.

The cost of eternal life is death.

You suck the bread from my marrow and in its stead spit out my un-tomorrow.

I fell like a hummingbird in an eagle's vortex and like a hare I reel in the lion's roar.

As I daydream in living color my goggles all askew. I seek the seam of things to come and dream a daydream mind boggling new.

An Earth flag: mono-global and mono-political?

On his way to one more good fuck he lay a spleen upon a meadow larking at the ploy of all the lachrymals to come.

Joe Zoa.

Beautifully mad.

Rocky is sick.

Death is the great One's last gift.

I am a slave and my master is poetry.

God is just a bunch of stars.

What comes tomorrow I do not say...a force beyond has strategized it for us.

Step out of your mold.

Loosing is beautiful.

Wined calves groom the sheen of hypocrisy's silver screen.

Reality is not reality anymore.

Tonight the world is dreaming an orgy such as kings and queens and potentates could not dream of in their wildest dreams.

My vulnerability hardens me.

Speak the words that are a gift.

A separate reality akin to reality.

When required by circumstances burning a flag is an act of extraordinary patriotism.

The enemies of heaven are on Earth.

Prometheus was changed into a rock and put on the edge of heaven.

Without children there is not a world.

There are flowers in one's heart.

Lithium, sodium, potassium, rubidium, cesium and francium.

In time did sentience dwell to grace with transient bonds the chariot's furious wheels.

Velcro armpits gather fuzz.

The star in a ballet is the ballet itself.

The food of the spirit of children is peace of mind.

The computer is a new crystal ball.

Love is a skill.

The carbon cycle, the solar carbon cycle, the stellar carbon cycle and the carbonic life thereof.

I feel like an embryo in a shell.

Like viruses in the microbia of silicon chips grand ideas slip by.

In cemeteries the wicked and the good lie side by side the Earth itself; their cairn.

Practice all temptations.

The tyranny of religion facilitates the tyranny of the state.

The Pope and George Bush can't compete with eternity.

We are golden-ringed diadems in a cobalt of nothingness.

Corporate totalitarianism..

TV is ugly, radio is a sham, public opinion is reactionary, the press lies; that is the media, the medium and the message.

Once a year I feel Victoriated.

Art is true religion.

My soul is not a hat that can hang on a religious peg.

75 million children work as slaves in South East Asia, 8 million are branded with irons.

The finger of blame points everywhere.

I grew up on TV's Hollywood sleaze. It helped me drop hypocritical religion and American values.

You can't hide the countenance of man...even in a limousine.

A single breath is like ten fingers.

If Zarathustra met Edith Piaf!

You are here.

Vive la décadence.

Let's leave well enough together.

God has billions of children stranded on a planet he forgot he made.

The glaucous heron's gorgeous laugh screams through a night's bristling air.

How many millimeters between inner and outer consciousness.

Neither heaven nor man will bear the rage of life on Earth.

Remedios Varo.

Society is a bad dream.

There is a wry sort of humor in stating the obvious with eloquence.

In truth they crush nuts in a cybernetic press

There are no golden nickels.

Roc: the greatest bird.

It's beautiful but it stinks.

The secret agent of time secures the sleep of devils.

Phobic sentimentality.

As I opened the book the noise of the words burst out as if I had stretched an accordion.

The man who saw time stand still stood still.

Power illegally gained by the political subversion of democratic societies is the M O of Capitalists.

Water water everywhere and every drop poisonous.

Evangelical capitalism.

Forget the contumacious rancor, tear up the affidavits, fire the judge for contempt of the populace, throw the rich out with the bath water.

An intellectual euphoria.

There is also guilt in the feeling that one is doing the right thing.

History does not have for a final purpose to bring humankind to understand him/herself.

Money phobia.

Private wealth is planetary murder.

St. Paul was an agent of Rome

Saint Hood was the brother of Robin Hood.

She was so lovely she escaped the velocity of my preconceptions.

Reality is indestructible.

Long live propaganda?

One moon same as 14 sake moons.

How cut the rough out of 20 centuries of hatred?

One must keep in mind that it is sane people who drive people insane.

Time is a portion of light.

Very soon later.

The devil loves good rules.

Art is created in an erotic state of mind.

The media are cans of worms.

Why worry about problems that belong to other people.

Mankind's eternal memories are not displaced by fashionable notions.

My life is like an umbrella when I open it it rains.

Between duvet-laden thighs I slept remembering infinity.

I don't give a shit about rich people who are generous.

Birds are all of one mind unfortunately they all have to share it.

Madness has a shorter spell than political agendas.

Le jour est devenu la nuit.

I weep day and night for the children of the planet.

We are all involved in an ignominious political dialectic.

To live in a world of imagination beyond imagination.

A spiral consciousness swallows itself in the nothingness.

Even Shakespeare could not do justice to reality.

A blue ribbon sperm count competition.

The mind of western man is stuck in green bullshit.

It is so sad we could almost laugh.

We are all soldiers fighting a sordid economic war against each other and the kids are alone at home.

Greetings to the ancestors as living and dying are one life goes on.

Children are holistic.

We are dealing with systematic bureaucratic dysfunction.

Eating flesh is porkitude.

My heart was broken all over the place.

You really have to be enlightened to eat tofu baloney.

Poetry is a language synergistic with heaven.

O Monde ton astuce sefface.

The evil force must be emasculated.

There is no dust like stardust.

To bring the mountain to its foot.

Poverty is a curable social disease.

It is still 1984.

The plottings of humankind are seen beyond Jupiter.

A fistful of words is a ton of dynamite.

Many thoughts, many places, fast food.

A trail of cherry blossoms has led me to the mountaintop.

Will there be different life forms and species on Earth 1000 million years from now?

On the chair one flower left behind.

On my birthday I would eat sushi and steamed clams.

From a part one can see that the whole is very funny.

A steering wheel is no good without a car.

Some find happiness in wealth others in a Haiku.

In silence a thunderous voice in noise a great deafness.

A silence fills the hall in space one sound.

The broad strokes of the swimmer make barely a ripple.

Faces in the frost pearls in a mirror.

Politicians hang around like coils of garlic sausage.

At the end of the four paths one direction.

Life is a glandular speculation.

There is a bad sign that is a good sign.

We shall become sparkling plasma.

The works of a fanatic are fanatical but the works of a just human are munificent.

How can a society that has so much be so empty.

The credibility gap is incredible.

For the Cities of Heaven language is the coin of the realm.

You can see in their eyes that their heart is dirty and that they can little love and then only if it serves their purpose.

Bozos are the mainstay of the human species.

Yuppies are rich bozos.

The Chinese are the oldest people on Earth, their ancestors lived in the days of the giants.

Dying is a great thing and everyone returns to one's own design.

A generation ready to die, careless of life and born to a fiery time.

What was left will become right again.

Escalate defeat.

Everything is made of real stuff remade into not real stuff.

Viruses like an Egyptian plague shall destroy the dangerous life form that now proudly stands upon this Earth weapons in hand.

And re-seed Mars with the offspring of a migrant earth.

Sometime I feel like jumping inside the window.

Ideas are my greatest addiction after imaginary sex.

Booze and drugs are by far much less harmful than right-wing politicians.

Sports are a pagan sacrament.

Love is in like a dream and out like a nightmare.

The only thing that shyness has done for me is to have made me brave. Where is Allah sleeping tonight?

For too many states the security of their elite is at the cost of the security of its citizens.

Our children are at the bottom of this pile of adult immaturity.

A glass full of clouds.

Rational suicide.

Social suicide.

Ideas like sand castles escape our grasp.

Sexuality is meant to be in a sense stream.

Rome was not un built in a day.

Still they procreated knowing their children would be enslaved and die.

My heart bursts when I see the cormorants of Siwash rock stare out to sea like litigious philosophers worried about the fate of species in that splendid deep.

Cute, coy and cryptic she beckoned me from the depth of cybernia...

a goddess drooling to be born.

Like leaves in the wind words flew off his face.

The bad shed an awful pall on the good.

The evening expanded beyond the pale of its dimensions.

Unlike the dinosaurs we exceed our ecosystem by the size of our mind.

No will can withstand the currents of time.

Matter is not as hard to mend as men's mind.

Soon there shall be no Bikinis Atoll.

Right-wing political sand castles.

The last big fuck is when you get laid to rest.

In Canada at the end of the second millennium children were born under bridges.

A creature self prophesied, a demon gone mad.

We are a sweet grass a ribonucleic sugar fart.

The righting politician stood still in front of the silent crowd his silk suit shining.

A force beyond us has strategized our tomorrow.

The he and the she is a product of it.

Vulnerability is a hardener.

The genderfication of post industrial societies.

Say the words that speak the gift.

Banality par excellence.

We must wash away the sins of our ancestors.

A separate reality so kin to it that it is kin to reality.

And we must surely wonder to what end are destined the self chosen?

The antediluvian Koi dreams below the sea its flesh waiting to be born.

It's god let's eat it.

The mind agonized with the ecstatic grief of creativity.

Destiny is a piece of cake.

The truth is in orbit.

Anonymostly.

The arch-bitchup of Cranberry.

He received both his amanuensis and his emulation at the same time.

Life is caught in the universe's mousetrap.

He pulled hats out of a rabbit's ass.

The McGospel according to McMoney: And McJesus said unto them: "I am from McGod." And McGhost went back and fifth between them. He was then McNailed to the McCross and McMary McWept for McHim.

To draw a new circle about the deep and re-circumscribe the human universe.

The word has been politically adulterated.

Pyrrhic hypnosis.

It is perverse to see things morally.

She came in a cloud of gold dust.

Longstraw a chief of staff.

Born to love I have loosed my mind in vain.

Fields and fields of alovera gel.

Foolhardy and braggadocios he stood eloquent and disheveled.

He passed water and left this world like a saint in an ablutionary.

I loved her crooked coccyx and bulbous breasts.

Beings are protected by their gelatinous affection.

Artists are true terrestrials.

Lost in death's grip and five hundred kilos of guilt.

On his deathbed, he said that the grass is always greener on the other side.

She sways before me like a giant neutrabank arousing desires deeper than the sea.

Moralism is a madness imposed on deviates.

And now time having come again upon itself weaves a path new to it but still foretold.

The best party is the one you have with yourself.

The universe recycles itself.

People relate to themselves according to the spirit of the universe.

A belly button is a part time job.

Sheep rams myths.

To love people is the greatest human responsibility.

The way I see it my computer has a lot less memory than I do even when I don't feel so good.

The wind speaks with the breath of a crowd and says quit pushing.

The wind catapults trough the skyscrapers.

P Ace's have a glitch complex.

The one person you do not listen to is yourself.

They spoke with a lot of Haiku-men.

A shogun wind blows its hyperbola in the coils of a historical breath.

It takes an artist to enjoy art. No artist creates all arts and many artists create no art.

Art is a human proclivity…an appendix. A remnant of spiritual origins.

I worry sometimes that god might be bored so I sometimes put flowers on the kitchen table.

How many individuals have four letter words killed?

Swearing is healthier than the morality that censures it.

Intellectual magnetism.

The music foamed below our consciousness.

Nature is seismographic.

I was thinking of everything at once when time and space exploded.

I hear the hooves of time thundering ahead.

God is the global collective consciousness.

The English reforms, the American devolution, the French revolution, the Russian and Chinese communist revolts, thus thus thus and thus the masses rise.

Vertical columns of blue light flash and shimmer ominously pointing to a coming eclipse of the sun.

My offspring flew off like a swan to another wonderland a continent away.

Meditating on a font, I sought a strange daydreaming while following the cursor.

What Humpty said to Dumpty: Having a highly tuned predisposition to reality I have had to philosophize so as to mend the praxis of my impossible conclusion; "We are all McDamned!.

I meditate on reality and it happens.

Exotic minute shadows preen in the frosted glass.

My thoughts are like such wild beasts that the Pleiades and the Hebrides echo with my singular dreaming.

With more energy than the physical can use the mind mines

As I in present dreaminess dream of a reality inverted and of time slowed to a standstill until it becomes as I dream of...

I was lost in a sea of incommensurable ambiguities.

Time has scored Space.

The oppressed have the hardest job on Earth.

A U: The gold was not so much in the hills after all it was in the gleam of dreams shinning off the face of solidified eternity.

He felt so guilty after foundling a bee that he slipped off the sidewalk and ruptured his spleen.

Le petit garçon roucoule comme une perdrix.

I walked into the dead heat of silence. I lay there on the floor in a state of grief my root drive unable to boot.

We should take the North and South poles and shove em.

Oh, the Guano of it all.

Holistically perfumed they bowed down before Zod.

It was something to look forward to even in retrospect.

They stand there…with virtual memory.

It was a hot cold war after all and Yankee Doodle sang the tune.

Religion is organized spiritual crime.

The weasels listened to a ratsody.

The Earth is made of fire, water, cheese and wine.

Psycho-physio-chemical Earthlings.

Engrossed in the fine print he lost his zeal for both details and the overall picture of things.

And the story ends when I am cold.

There was Cro-Magnon man now there is pro-magnum man.

Questions are the command prompt of intellect and the M O of social evolution.

It was a unique phenomenon and a sine qua non for the specified criterion.

Gala's system file is not rebootable.

And to learn despite the sheer genius of one's natural proclivity.

Radiance = radiation.

He took the Oat of office.

Language is the syntax of the command prompt of times.

I wrote an orgasm.

Oh, Romeo Romeo where is your portfolio.

Humanity is a virus.

The data is lost in the datum.

In the beginning was the beginning and the beginning never stopped even after the End the beginning continued to become world without end.

www.ingramcontent.com/pod-product-compliance
Lightning Source LLC
Chambersburg PA
CBHW041131110526
44592CB00020B/2760